SEASONS
IN GOD'S WORLD

written by
Beverly Beckmann

illustrated by
Carolyn Ewing Bowser

CONCORDIA®

Publishing House
St. Louis

God made the world and all that is in it.

Then He rested for one day.
People rest on one day, too.

On that day of rest, people go to church.
Sometimes they go to church on other special days, too.

**The calendar tells us
what day it is and when to go to church.**

**In fall, we go to church through the crisp leaves,
and we feel cool breezes on our faces.**

At church, we thank God for all the good food that grows in the farmer's field.

In winter, we go to church in colder weather. Sometimes it is snowing.

In winter, we hear at church that Baby Jesus was born. Jesus' birthday is called Christmas.

It is on December 25.

**In spring, we go to church
and look for baby birds and wait for seeds to grow.**

In church, we hear that Jesus died on the cross.

The day Jesus died is called Good Friday.

On Easter Sunday, we hear that Jesus did not stay dead. He was alive again.

On Ascension Thursday, we hear that Jesus went into heaven.

On Pentecost Sunday, we hear about the Holy Spirit. He helps us love Jesus.

In summer, we walk to church in hot weather and bright sunlight,

and we thank God for seasons and special church days.

Dear family members,

Nursery-age children have a difficult time understanding that which cannot be touched or seen. They can learn the names of the days and months and can recognize a calendar when seen. But children really cannot understand the concept of years and seasons until about age six or seven.

Therefore, for preschoolers, lay the groundwork for later, fuller understanding. Point out the names of the days; talk about the number of days until a birthday; use pictures to discuss the weather changes in your particular climate. These approaches will help your child sense the feeling of a particular season and its relation to other seasons.

More important, relate the festivals of the church year to the seasons. This will help the child understand that God has a plan for His world and for our salvation.

Beverly Beckmann

Beverly Beckmann